Investor-State Dispute Settlement

A Reality Check

AF873571

Authors
Scott Miller
Gregory N. Hicks

A Report of the CSIS Scholl Chair in International Business

January 2015

CSIS | CENTER FOR STRATEGIC & INTERNATIONAL STUDIES

ROWMAN & LITTLEFIELD
Lanham • Boulder • New York • London

About CSIS

For over 50 years, the Center for Strategic and International Studies (CSIS) has worked to develop solutions to the world's greatest policy challenges. Today, CSIS scholars are providing strategic insights and bipartisan policy solutions to help decisionmakers chart a course toward a better world.

CSIS is a nonprofit organization headquartered in Washington, D.C. The Center's 220 full-time staff and large network of affiliated scholars conduct research and analysis and develop policy initiatives that look into the future and anticipate change.

Founded at the height of the Cold War by David M. Abshire and Admiral Arleigh Burke, CSIS was dedicated to finding ways to sustain American prominence and prosperity as a force for good in the world. Since 1962, CSIS has become one of the world's preeminent international institutions focused on defense and security; regional stability; and transnational challenges ranging from energy and climate to global health and economic integration.

Former U.S. senator Sam Nunn has chaired the CSIS Board of Trustees since 1999. Former deputy secretary of defense John J. Hamre became the Center's president and chief executive officer in April 2000.

CSIS does not take specific policy positions; accordingly, all views expressed herein should be understood to be solely those of the author(s).

© 2015 by the Center for Strategic and International Studies. All rights reserved.

ISBN 978-1-4422-4072-8 (pb); 978-1-4422-4073-5 (eBook)

Disclaimer: the views expressed in this report are those of the authors and do not necessarily represent the views of the U.S. Department of State or the U.S. government.

Center for Strategic & International Studies
1616 Rhode Island Avenue, NW
Washington, DC 20036
202-887-0200 | www.csis.org

Rowman & Littlefield
4501 Forbes Boulevard
Lanham, MD 20706
301-459-3366 | www.rowman.com

Contents

Acknowledgments

The authors would like to give special thanks to CSIS and its corporate sponsors for their generous support of this project.

We would also like to thank Laura Collins for her exemplary research and analytical contributions to this report. We would also like to thank our colleagues in the CSIS Publications Department, led by James Dunton and Alison Bours, for their editing and design work on this report.

The following advisory panel is recognized for their invaluable contributions to this project. By participating in roundtable discussions and offering comments on numerous drafts, they have played an indispensable role in shaping this report.

These experts participated in an individual capacity, not on behalf of the institutions they represent. Individual participants do not necessarily endorse every recommendation.

Steve Canner

Lee Caplan

Marney Cheek

Paul H. DeLaney III

Linda Dempsey

Shaun Donnelly

Charles Freeman

Eva Hampl

Sean Heather

Dorothy Hoffman

Steve Jacobs

Jonathan S. Kallmer

Locke Loeb

Ted Posner

Wes Scholz

Michael Smart

Executive Summary

Investor-state dispute settlement (ISDS), a provision in bilateral investment treaties (BITs) and other international investment agreements that allows investors to enter arbitration with states over treaty breaches, has become controversial in the United States and our negotiating partners. Critics, including some governments, have argued that ISDS is unnecessary while others insist it is illegitimate as public policy.

This report is an empirical review of ISDS, based on the record of disputes under existing investment treaties. The key findings are as follows:

- Over 90 percent of the nearly 2,400 BITs in force have operated without a single investor claim of a treaty breach.
- The number of disputes filed in the past 10 years has increased. Overall, the rise in disputes has been proportional to the rise in outward foreign capital stock. There are more disputes, but there are also more investors and more capital invested abroad.
- Investors from large capital-exporting economies are active users of ISDS. European countries are a party to over 1,200 BITs and account for 46 percent of global foreign direct investment (FDI) stock; in the past decade European investors have filed more than half of investment arbitration claims. Similarly, the United States is responsible for 24 percent of outward FDI stock; U.S. investors have filed 22 percent of ISDS claims.
- Many disputes arise in economic sectors characterized by high levels of state intervention. About 40 percent of filed ISDS claims are in oil, gas, mining, and power generation, sectors that often feature prominent state involvement.
- Disputes are also most frequent in states with weak legal institutions. Argentina (53 claims) and Venezuela (36 claims) are the leading respondent states.
- About a third of ISDS cases are settled in advance of a ruling. For disputes that end in an arbitral decision, states win about twice as often as investors. When investors do prevail, awards are a small fraction of the initial claim—on average, less than 10 cents on the dollar.

Investors generally recognize that ISDS is expensive and time-consuming, on par with complex civil litigation. While arbitration offers neutrality and finality, investors are typically aware of the low likelihood of prevailing and the risk that filing a claim presents to their future operations.

Many of the criticisms of ISDS are overblown. Some claim that ISDS gives investors "special rights," yet most treaty protections are identical to universal civil rights accorded most citizens. Further, critics exaggerate the notion that investors "sue to overturn regulations"; BITs explicitly limit awards to monetary damages. Finally, conflating ISDS with “big corporations” ignores that most U.S. investors who have filed investment arbitration claims are individuals or firms with fewer than 500 employees.

Treaty-based investment protection represents a major advance in the fair treatment of aliens and the peaceful resolution of disputes. Given the alternatives, withdrawing from investment treaties—the logical conclusion of the critics’ position—would likely have negative consequences for economic growth and the rule of law.

Introduction

Bilateral investment treaties (BITs) are international agreements between two economies that set forth binding rules on each government's treatment of investment from the other economy. The basic rules are similar to core principles of U.S. law and policy and are an established and recognized component of international investment law that require governments to: not discriminate in favor of home-country or third-country investors; afford investors' investments fair and equitable treatment and full protection and security; provide full and prompt, adequate, and effective compensation in the event of an expropriation; allow investors to move their capital into and out of the country; not impose performance requirements (such as local content requirements); and allow for neutral arbitration of disputes if treaty obligations are breached. Nearly 2,400 BITs and similar agreements are in force worldwide,[1] including investment chapters in free-trade agreements and plurilateral arrangements like the Energy Charter Treaty.

The operation and effect of dispute settlement arrangements for investment agreements are different from trade agreements. A typical trade dispute affects the treatment of a class of goods or services originating from a party, usually not the product or service of a single firm, although such claims have been filed. Most trade agreements contain state-to-state dispute settlement procedures and the remedy for a trade dispute is usually prospective, and often requires the losing party to modify the terms of trade (e.g., laws, regulations, and/or tariff rate) for the good in question.

However, BITs provide protections that extend to a firm, and a breach of treaty obligations affects an individual enterprise. BITs allow a foreign investor to bring a claim in arbitration directly against the host state for a breach in the terms of an agreement, against the government responsible for the breach—thus, "investor-state dispute settlement," or ISDS. For investment disputes, the remedy is retrospective, typically in the form of compensation to make an investor whole following a breach of the agreement—ISDS arbitrators cannot require a state to change its laws and regulations.

Since trade and investment agreements are debated and ratified by signatory governments in keeping with their procedures for ratification, ISDS provisions in such agreements are expressions of national policy in the same ways as any other statutes, regulations, or other measures approved by governments.

Challenges to the Legitimacy of BITs

As the number of disputes filed by investors has increased over the past 10–15 years, so has the controversy surrounding the inclusion of ISDS in trade agreements and investment treaties. Recent criticisms of BITs and ISDS have led some governments to reexamine their policies toward foreign investors with a few questioning whether investment agreements with ISDS are necessary, or in the interest of host states. For instance, Indonesia and South Africa, both large capital importers, but also emerging

[1] UN Conference on Trade and Development (UNCTAD), "Investment Policy Hub: International Investment Agreements Navigator," http://investmentpolicyhub.unctad.org/IIA.

regional capital exporters, have announced high-profile decisions stating their intent to allow existing investment agreements containing ISDS to expire, arguing that domestic laws and regulations related to investment have evolved to the point where existing ISDS provisions are now irrelevant.[2] In addition, Ecuador and Venezuela have withdrawn officially from the Convention on the Settlement of Investment Disputes between States and Nationals of Other States. Other governments that were once active in negotiating new BITs now take the position that ISDS is not needed in some agreements, based on their opinions about existing domestic legal standards being sufficient to resolve disputes, such as under the 2004 U.S.-Australia Free Trade Agreement, which contains an investment chapter without ISDS. Overall, fewer new BITs are being negotiated, and many major economies—both capital importers and capital exporters—are reconsidering their policies.

Beyond changing attitudes among governments, nongovernmental critics of ISDS often place the blame for the controversy on the behavior of investors and argue that ISDS undermines domestic law by prioritizing investor preferences over government policy. Some criticism of ISDS centers on the rising number of disputes. Many nongovernment organizations (NGOs) argue that ISDS should be abandoned entirely, and foreign investors should instead rely on host-country courts or state-to-state dispute resolution.

These critics argue that BITs and ISDS give foreign investors "special rights" unavailable to domestic firms, and undermine state sovereignty by offering a means for investors to intimidate host governments to change policies arrived at through the democratic process. NGOs often sound the alarm about a "growing" number of ISDS "cases," and the "enormous" amounts investors are claiming as compensation. Lori Wallach, director of Public Citizen's Global Trade Watch, argues that BITs "allow companies to challenge public interest regulations outside of domestic court systems before tribunals of three private sector trade attorneys operating under minimal to no conflict of interest rules. These arbitrators can order governments to pay corporations unlimited taxpayer-funded compensation for having to comply with policies that affect their future expected profits, and with which domestic investors have to comply."[3] Ska Keller, member of the European Parliament representing the European Greens, wrote that "[d]emocratic decision-making is forcefully going under the knife through international arbitration. The accused states have only two options: either they can be like others and take back the decisions they have made, or they can pay huge sums in compensation to the investor."[4] Daniel J. Ikenson of the Cato Institute writes that "ISDS turns national treatment on its head, giving privileges to foreign companies that are not available to domestic companies."[5]

---

[2] Ben Bland and Shawn Donnan, "Indonesia to terminate more than 60 bilateral investment treaties," *Financial Times*, March 26, 2014, http://www.ft.com/intl/cms/s/0/3755c1b2-b4e2-11e3-af92-00144feabdc0.html#axzz3NK0O7u6u.

[3] Lori Wallach, "Announcement of Flawed 2012 Model BIT Shows Agenda Motivating Obama TPP [Trans-Pacific Partnership] Talks," Public Citizen, April 20, 2012, http://citizen.typepad.com/eyesontrade/2012/04/announcement-of-flawed-investment-rules-show-agenda-motivating-obama-trade-talks.html.

[4] Ska Keller, "Investor-state lawsuits threaten democracy," TTIP [Transatlantic Trade and Investment Partnership]: Beware What Lies Beneath, March 26, 2014, http://ttip2014.eu/blog-detail/blog/Ska%20Keller%20Investors%20TTIP.html.

[5] Daniel J. Ikenson, "A Compromise to Advance the Trade Agenda: Purge Negotiations of Investor-State Dispute Settlement," Cato Institute, March 4, 2014, http://www.cato.org/publications/free-trade-bulletin/compromise-advance-trade-agenda-purge-negotiations-investor-state.

Some elected officials have responded to these criticisms with proposals to narrow the scope of treaty protections in ways that limit and in some disputes eliminate the ability of investors to file claims. Some proposals along these lines were included in the 2004 U.S. Model BIT. It also appears that the scope of coverage in the Comprehensive Economic and Trade Agreement (CETA) is much less than previous European or Canadian BITs as well as the U.S. Model BIT. Nevertheless, Germany's economy minister, Sigmar Gabriel, said in September 2014 that his country would not approve the CETA agreement unless its ISDS provisions are scrapped.[6] Other reform ideas include creation of an appellate mechanism, such as the one the U.S. Congress mandated in the United States-Central America-Dominican Republic Free Trade Agreement (CAFTA). Still others have proposed mandating alternative dispute-resolution mechanisms that would precede initiation of an ISDS filing. If such trends prevail, foreign investors will become wholly dependent upon host-country regulators and courts, some of which are in countries with nondemocratic governments and poor rule of law track records.

A Reality Check

Despite these criticisms, our research suggests that BITs represent an important contribution to the rule of law and provide benefits to both capital importers and capital exporters, with nearly 90 percent of all BITs in force operating without a single dispute.[7] Further, while there are more disputes now than in the past, the growth in investment disputes is proportionate to the rise in foreign-invested capital stock, which reached US$25 trillion in 2013.[8] These investments are owned by 80,000 multinational enterprises, which in turn own approximately 100,000 affiliates in countries around the world.[9]

There is further evidence that the system is working to the benefit of all parties when looking at the record of completed disputes: about one-third of disputes are settled without arbitrators reaching a decision; in disputes that reach a decision, investors win only about one-third of the time; and awards are generally pennies on the dollar claimed. Finally, ISDS can be viewed as a last resort for investors given the low winning percentage, high arbitration costs, the current interest in a going concern, risks to relationships with host-country governments, and opportunities for future investment.

The network of BITs that has developed over the past half-century represents a great achievement in the fair treatment of aliens and the peaceful resolution of disputes between parties. The extension of treaty-based protections lowers risk associated with international investment, which facilitates economic growth and job creation. Access to neutral arbitration helps de-politicize disputes. The success of BITs and ISDS in creating a predictable environment for investors has contributed to prosperity in a number of ways, and should not be abandoned without serious consideration of the alternatives.

---

[6] "Germany Wants Investment Clause Scrapped in EU-Canada Trade Deal," EurActiv, September 25, 2014. http://www.euractiv.com/sections/trade-industry/germany-wants-investment-clause-scrapped-eu-canada-trade-deal-308717.

[7] Investment Treaty Arbitration (ITA), "Investment Treaties," http://www.italaw.com/cases/by-treaty; and UNCTAD, "Investment Policy Hub: International Investment Agreements Navigator.

[8] UNCTAD, *World Investment Report, 2014: Investing in the Sustainable Development Goals* (Geneva: UNCTAD, 2014), 209, http://unctad.org/en/PublicationsLibrary/wir2014_en.pdf.

[9] W. Michael Reisman, "International Investment Arbitration and ADR [Alternative Dispute Resolution]: Married but Best Living Apart," *ICSID* [International Centre for Settlement of Investment Disputes] *Review* 24, no. 1 (2009): 186, http://www.law.yale.edu/documents/pdf/sela/Reisman_reading.pdf.

Do BITs Convey "Special Rights" to Foreign Investors?

The rights provided by BITs and investment chapters of trade agreements—fair and equitable treatment, full protection and security, no expropriation without compensation, and access to impartial arbitration—are consistent with the universal civil rights at the core of most democracies. U.S. BIT provisions are modeled after the takings clause of the U.S. Constitution, which states that "No person shall be . . . deprived of . . . property, without due process of law; nor shall property be taken for public use, without just compensation."[1] Similarly, European BIT obligations are consistent with Article I of the Protocol to the European Convention for the Protection of Human Rights and Fundamental Freedoms, which states that "No one shall be deprived of his possessions except in the public interest and subject to the conditions provided by law and by the general principles of international law."[2] More broadly, Article 17 of the UN's Universal Declaration of Human Rights says that "Everyone has the right to own property alone as well as in association with others," and "No one shall be arbitrarily deprived of his property." Article 10 of the Universal Declaration adds that "Everyone is entitled in full equality to a fair and public hearing by an independent and impartial tribunal, in the determination of his rights. . . ."[3]

U.S. and European BITs guarantee that their foreign investors will receive what are essentially universal rights and protections from treaty partners. Meanwhile, based on the international legal principle of reciprocity, BITs grant the same rights to foreign investors locating in the United States or Europe, including impartial dispute settlement. While some assert that courts in developed economies are sufficiently independent and impartial that ISDS is unnecessary, two recent European studies of ISDS have noted that "neither U.S. federal nor state law fully protects foreign investors from discrimination." Both studies added that "investment cases such as Loewen suggest that U.S. courts, and especially civil juries, may be biased against foreigners."[4]

---

[1] Library of Congress, *The Constitution of the United States of America: Analysis and Interpretation* (Washington, DC: U.S. Government Printing Office, 1996), 1273, http://www.gpo.gov/fdsys/pkg/GPO-CONAN-1992/pdf/GPO-CONAN-1992.pdf.
[2] European Court of Human Rights, *European Convention on Human Rights* (Strasbourg: European Court of Human Rights, June 2010), 31, http://www.echr.coe.int/Documents/Convention_ENG.pdf.
[3] United Nations, "The Universal Declaration of Human Rights," 2014, http://www.un.org/en/documents/udhr/index.shtml#a10.
[4] "The 'I' in TTIP: Why the Transatlantic Trade and Investment Partnership Needs an Investment Chapter," Federation of German Industries, BDI Document no. 9, September 2014, 26, http://www.bdi.eu/download_content/Globalisierung MaerkteUndHandel/BDI_The_I_in__TTIP_140930.pdf; and Christian Tietje and Freya Baetens, "The Impact of Investor-State-Dispute Settlement (ISDS) in the Transatlantic Trade and Investment Partnership," June 24, 2014, 8, http://www.investmentpolicycentral.com/sites/g/files/g798796/f/201409/the-impact-of-investor-state-dispute-settlement-isds-in-the-ttip%20%281%29.pdf.

How BITs and ISDS Became the Standard for Investment Protection

The Bilateral Investment Treaty represents a major advance in the treatment of foreign investors. While today's system is easy to take for granted, the current levels of legal protection accorded to foreign investors is a recent, welcome development. Prior to the emergence of BITs, foreign investors had to rely on their own governments to recover losses from a foreign government's expropriation or other mistreatment of assets. Frequently, more powerful states intervened diplomatically or militarily to protect the economic interests of their nationals. In the first 160 years of its existence, the U.S.

military intervened in foreign countries 88 times to protect Americans' private commercial interests.[10] The practice was first glorified and then vilified as "gunboat diplomacy." Whether or not force of arms was used, the political dimension of state-to-state disputes was a fact of life.

The pre-BIT era presented substantive and process concerns for investors. According to the United Nations, the 14 years prior to the entry into force of the first BIT saw 875 government takings of foreign investor property in 62 countries for which there was no effective remedy.[11] International law offered no consensus: in 1964, for example, the U.S. Supreme Court observed that "there are few if any issues in international law today on which opinion seems to be so divided as the limitations on a state's power to expropriate the property of aliens."[12] When it came to process, foreign investors could seek the support of their governments through their espousal of a particular claim only after "exhaust[ing] all host nation legal remedies."[13] This meant a time-consuming, unpredictable adventure through local courts with suspect impartiality. On rare occasions, espousal and adjudication before the International Court of Justice produced a favorable outcome for an investor, but usually a potential case would languish as higher diplomatic priorities pushed it aside until it faded into memory.

Two innovations changed this situation. The first was the substantive reform known as the modern BIT. The BIT was an advance over earlier treaties of Friendship, Commerce, and Navigation in that it explicitly bridged the gap between capital exporters and capital importers with respect to fair and equitable treatment, protections against uncompensated expropriation, and other features. The reform to the legal process was the establishment of the International Centre for Settlement of Investment Disputes (ICSID). The first modern BIT, between Germany and Pakistan, was concluded in 1959,[14] and since then nearly 2,400 BITs and similar instruments have entered into force.[15] The ICSID Convention entered into force in 1966, and today 159 economies are signatories.[16]

For the first time, states made binding commitments concerning the treatment of investors, the breach of which investors could refer directly to a neutral panel before which both parties would have equal legal status. The BIT with neutral arbitration in a rules-based facility gave foreign investors and states both rights and a remedy in one legal instrument, the adoption of which has positively altered the global international investment landscape.

---

[10] "Timeline of United States Military Operations," Wikipedia, http://en.wikipedia.org/wiki/Timeline_of_United_States_military_operations.
[11] Tietje and Baetens, "The Impact of Investor State Dispute Settlement (ISDS)," 21.
[12] Banco Nacional de Cuba v. Sabbatino, 376 U.S. 398 (1964).
[13] Ibid.
[14] Roderick Abbott et al., *Demystifying Investor-State Dispute Settlement (ISDS),*" ECIPE Occasional Paper No. 5/2014 (Brussels: European Centre for International Political Economy, May 2014), 4, http://www.ecipe.org/media/publication_pdfs/OCC52014__1.pdf.
[15] UNCTAD, Investment Policy Hub: International Investment Agreements Navigator."
[16] International Centre for Settlement of Investment Disputes (ICSID), "Member States," https://icsid.worldbank.org/apps/ICSIDWEB/about/Pages/Member-States.aspx.

Investor-State Dispute Settlement: Analyzing Filed Claims

The number of investor-state dispute settlement (ISDS) arbitrations has risen sharply, especially during the past 10 years. According to United Nations Conference on Trade and Development (UNCTAD), about 100 claims were initiated during the 15-year period 1987–2002, but from 2003 until 2013, the number of filed claims more than quadrupled, reaching a total of 568.[1] What are the characteristics of these claims, and what has contributed to the increased utilization of ISDS?

First, it is important to note that the vast majority of bilateral investment treaties (BITs) and BIT-like agreements have operated throughout their existence without a single claim being filed. Overall, over 90 percent of treaties are functioning with no treaty breaches alleged by investors. Essentially, the host government is acting in a way that treats foreign investors according to the terms of the treaty in most circumstances. Likewise, it is reasonable to assume in these situations that investors are also operating responsibly within the state's domestic legal system.

The most apparent reason for the rise in ISDS arbitrations is the concurrent rise in the stock of foreign direct investment (FDI). Since the beginning of the BIT era in 1959, the stock of global FDI has expanded faster than the growth of global economic output. In 1960, the global stock of FDI was US$60 billion,[2] just 4.4 percent of total world output of US$1.35 trillion, as measured by the World Bank.[3] As of 2013, the stock of global FDI exceeds US$25 trillion.[4] In simplest terms, ISDS claims are directly proportional to FDI stock, as long as most of the investment is covered by treaty protections. As shown in the graph below, the growth in ISDS claims and the growth in outward FDI stock follow a similar trend.

Further, and unsurprisingly, investors from economies that are large capital exporters are the most frequent filers of dispute claims. Europe is the source of 46 percent (US$12 trillion) of global outward FDI stock,[5] and European investors account for just over half (300) of all arbitration claims filed, with the Netherlands (61), the United Kingdom (42), and Germany (39) being the most frequent home states for claimants.[6] Similarly, the

---

[1] United Nations Conference on Trade and Development (UNCTAD), *World Investment Report, 2014: Investing in the SDGs* (Geneva: UNCTAD, 2014), 124, http://unctad.org/en/PublicationsLibrary/wir2014_en.pdf.
[2] Geoffrey Jones, "Restoring a Global Economy, 1950–1980," Harvard Business School, August 22, 2005, http://hbswk.hbs.edu/item/4961.html.
[3] Knoema, "GDP Statistics from the World Bank," November 2014, http://knoema.com/mhrzolg/gdp-statistics-from-the-world-bank#World.
[4] UNCTAD, *World Investment Report, 2014*, 209.
[5] Ibid.
[6] UNCTAD, "Investor-State Dispute Settlement: An Information Note on the United States and the European Union," IIA Issues Note, no. 2, June 2014, 8, http://unctad.org/en/PublicationsLibrary/webdiaepcb2014d4_en.pdf.

Figure 1: Growth in FDI vs. Growth in Investor-State Disputes

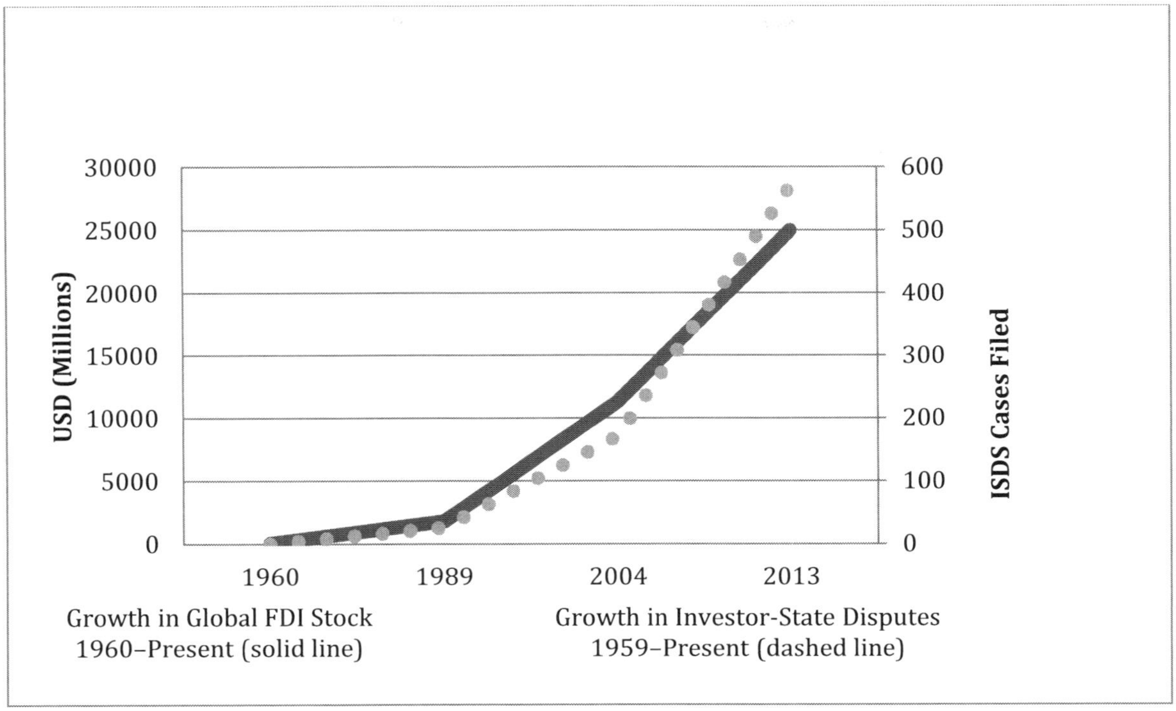

Figure 2: EU and U.S. FDI and ISDS Claims

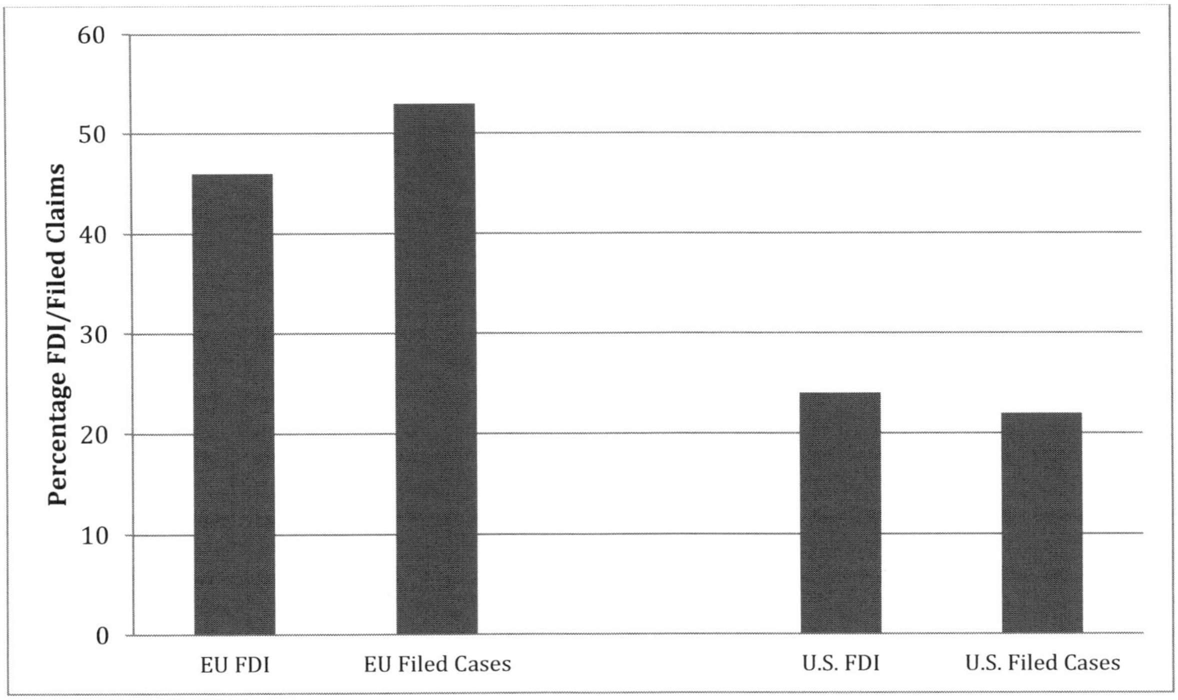

United States is the world's largest single country source of outward FDI, providing 24 percent of the capital stock (US$ 6.4 trillion)[7]; U.S. investors are also responsible for the largest individual share of ISDS claims (127, or 22 percent).[8] After the United States, the Netherlands, the United Kingdom, and Germany, the balance of the top 10 claimant source states are Canada (26), France (25), Italy (23), Spain (22), Turkey (18), and Switzerland (15).[9]

Next, disputes tend to occur in economic sectors with significant government involvement or those governments view as critical for the national economy. Looking just at ICSID-registered claims, over one-quarter of claims have been filed related to foreign investments in the oil, gas, and mining sectors. The electricity, power, and other energy sectors have experienced the second-highest proportion of disputes, 13 percent. Construction and finance are the third-highest sectors with 7 percent of disputes, while water, sanitation, and flood protection tie with the information and communication sectors with 6 percent of disputes each.

Finally, disputes tend to arise in host economies with poor rule-of-law records. Argentina has been the most frequent ISDS respondent state (53 ISDS claims, or 9 percent of all claims filed). Venezuela, with 36 claims filed against it, is the second on the list of states facing the largest number of claims.[10] These two countries are ranked 147th and 148th (out of 148 countries) in the World Economic Forum's Index on the Efficiency of Legal Framework in Challenging Regulations.[11] Rounding out the list of most frequent ISDS respondent states are the Czech Republic (28), Egypt (23), Ecuador (22), Canada (22), Mexico (21), Poland (17), the United States (16), and India, Kazakhstan, and Ukraine (15).[12] Transparency International's Corruption Perceptions Index, a commonly used mechanism for rating the governance performance of countries, shows that top claim attractors Argentina, Venezuela, Egypt, Ecuador, Mexico, India, Kazakhstan, and Ukraine all have relatively poor governance indicators.[13]

Wins, Awards, and Costs: Assessing ISDS Outcomes[14]

Our research indicates that states win the majority of cases. In the cases when investors win, tribunal damage awards are a fraction of the amounts investors claim. Additionally, costs for representation and administration are high and can exceed damages awarded if

[7] UNCTAD, *World Investment Report, 2014*, 210.
[8] UNCTAD, "Investor-State Dispute Settlement," 8.
[9] Ibid., 9.
[10] UNCTAD, "Recent Developments in Investor-State Dispute Settlement (ISDS)," IIA Issues Note, no. 1, April 2014, 8, http://unctad.org/en/PublicationsLibrary/webdiaepcb2014d3_en.pdf.
[11] Roderick Abbott et al., *Demystifying Investor-State Dispute Settlement (ISDS)*," ECIPE Occasional Paper No. 5/2014 (Brussels: European Centre for International Political Economy, May 2014), 11, http://www.ecipe.org/media/publication_pdfs/OCC52014__1.pdf.
[12] UNCTAD, "Recent Developments in Investor-State Dispute Settlement (ISDS)," 8.
[13] Transparency International, "Corruption Perceptions Index 2013," http://cpi.transparency.org/cpi2013/results/. Argentina, score = 36, rank = 106; Venezuela, score = 20, rank = 160; Czech Republic, score = 48, rank = 57; Egypt, score = 32, rank = 114; Ecuador, score = 35, rank = 102; Canada, score = 81, rank = 9; Mexico, score = 34, rank = 106; Poland, score = 60, rank = 38; United States, score = 73, rank = 19; India, score = 36, rank = 94; Kazakhstan, score = 26, rank = 140; Ukraine, score = 25, rank = 144.
[14] The three outcomes—investor win, state win, and settlement—are defined as follows for the purposes of this report: investors win when panels awarded them financial compensation; settlements are so indicated in the record; and the remaining outcomes are considered a win for the state.

Figure 3: ICSID ISDS Outcomes (all claims)

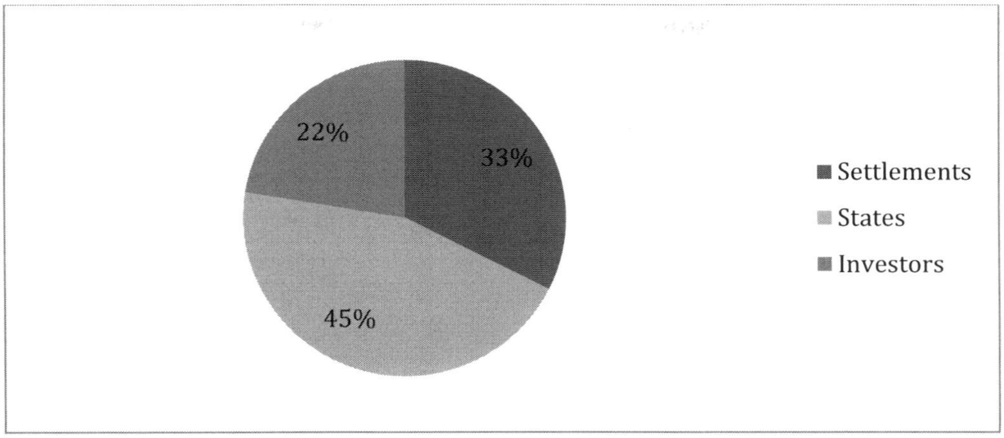

Figure 4: ICSID ISDS Outcomes (first 50 claims)

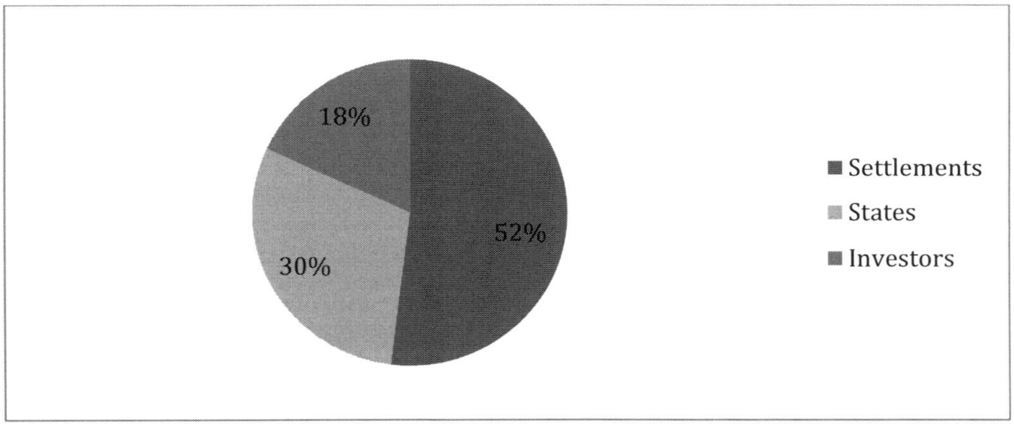

Figure 5: ICSID ISDS Outcomes (latest 50 claims)

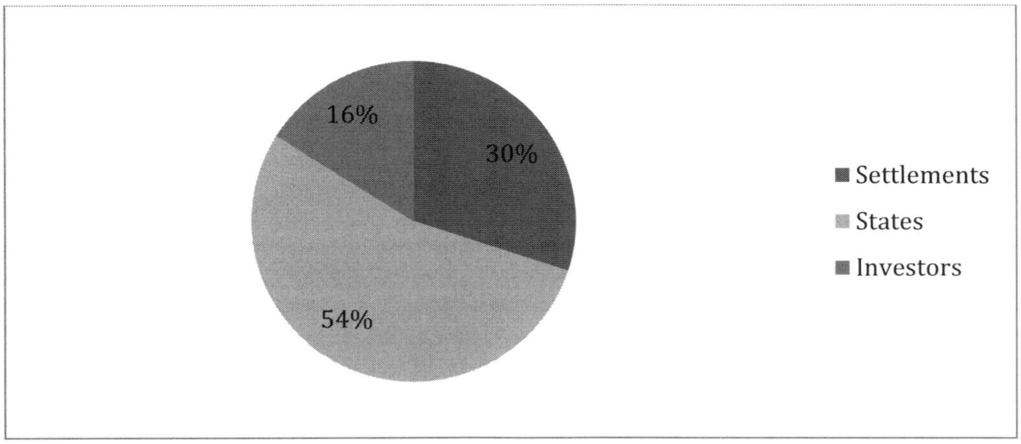

the claim is successful. Moreover, total costs of arbitration are difficult to predict, because arbitration systems have not established clear rules to allocate costs, and tribunals have addressed cost allocation differently.

Among the facilities for dispute settlement, ICSID, which is the facility of choice for three-fifths of disputes, provides to the public the most information about their resolution. Of the 288 disputes ICSID lists as completed, we could identify the results of 268 of those arbitrations.[15] ISDS arbitration disputes that have reached completion—through either settlement by the parties or decision by the arbitration panel—offer a more granular view of the costs and benefits of ISDS.

ICSID records show that 33 percent of claims (87 of 268) were settled by the parties before the arbitrators reached a decision.[16] For the remaining claims (181), we found that 67 percent of disputes (121) were resolved in favor of the respondent state, while only 33 percent (60) were decided in favor of the investor. The pattern was similar during the early years of ICSID arbitrations (1972–2001), except for a higher rate of settlements. Settlements were reached in 26 of the first 50 disputes, state respondents prevailed in 15, and investors won 9.[17]

An interesting finding relates to the size of the businesses involved in dispute settlement. While foreign investors are popularly thought of as "big business," the majority of U.S. claimants using the ICSID facility appear to be individuals or enterprises with fewer than 500 employees, designating them as "small and medium-sized enterprises" (SME), according to the U.S. Small Business Administration.[18] In the 105 disputes filed at ICSID by American investors, two-thirds of the participants in the arbitrations were individuals or SMEs. Disputes involving U.S. individuals or SMEs appear to reach a settlement less often than other claims: in 29 completed arbitrations, settlements were reached in only 4, while the state respondent prevailed in 19 disputes (65 percent) and investors won 6.

In terms of damages awarded, the record shows that while the amounts claimed by investors in their arbitration filings can be large, the amounts actually awarded are substantially less. In her initial empirical examination of 52 final ISDS awards, Professor Susan D. Franck found that the average claim was US$343.5 million, but the average damage award was only US$10.4 million, just three cents on the dollar of the amount originally claimed.[19] Similarly, damage claims in the 51 ICSID-resolved North American Free Trade Agreement (NAFTA) Chapter 11 disputes averaged US$2.9 billion, but the average damage award was US$66 million—just over two cents on the dollar. A subsequent expanded analysis of claims and awards through January 2012 showed

---

[15] International Centre for Settlement of Investment Disputes (ICSID), "List of Concluded Cases," https://icsid.worldbank.org/ICSID/FrontServlet?requestType=GenCaseDtlsRH&actionVal=ListConcluded; and ICSID, "Investment Treaty Arbitration," https://icsid.worldbank.org/apps/ICSIDWEB/cases/Pages/AdvancedSearch.aspx?cs=CD28.

[16] See also W. Michael Reisman, "International Investment Arbitration and ADR: Married but Best Living Apart," *ICSID Review* 24, no. 1 (2009): 187. "Once a dispute has reached the notice-of-arbitration state at ICSID, Eloise Obadia reports that 34% are even then still settled."

[17] ICSID, "List of Concluded Cases."

[18] U.S. Small Business Administration, "Table of Small Business Size Standards Matched to North American Industry Classification System Codes," July 2014, http://www.sba.gov/sites/default/files/Size_Standards_Table.pdf.

[19] Susan D. Franck, "Empirically Evaluating Claims about Investment Treaty Arbitration," *North Carolina Law Review* 86 (2007): 57–59.

Figure 6: SME ICSID Outcomes

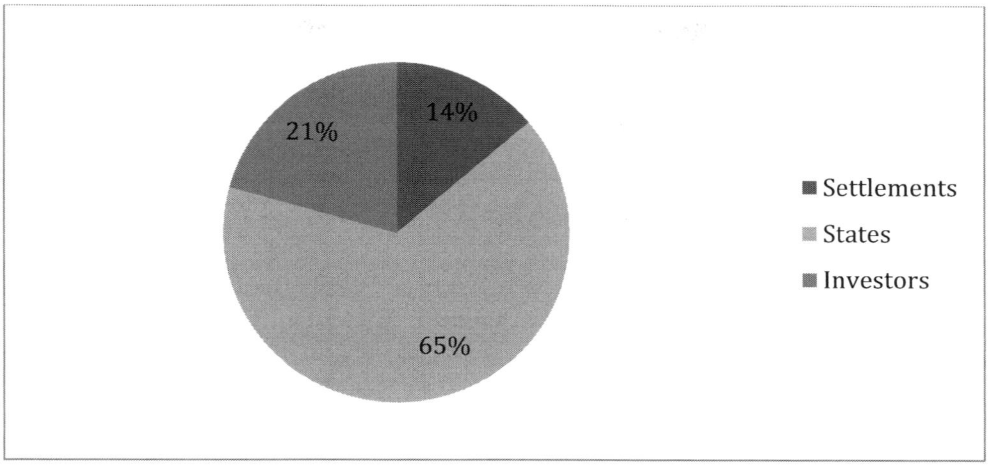

remarkable consistency with these results: the average amount claimed was US$622 million, and the average award was US$16.6 million, or just under three cents per dollar claimed.[20] This empirical work indicates that actual awards are proportional and that they represent no threat to "bankrupt" a country.

By comparison, the U.S. Court of Federal Claims awarded in the 2011–2012 case year an average of less than two cents per dollar claimed.[21] Given the high amounts at stake, the high arbitration costs, and information asymmetries, ISDS is more akin to forms of adjudication where parties should expect respondents to have a relative advantage. A better analogy for ISDS might therefore be claimant success in whistleblower lawsuits,[22] *qui tam* litigation (civil lawsuit brought by whistleblowers under the False Claims Act),[23] *Bivens* lawsuits against government officials for violations of citizens' U.S. constitutionalrights,[24] citizen complaints against agency action, civil or prisoner rights cases,[25] or medical malpractice litigation.[26] These categories are also somewhat

---

[20] Susan D. Franck, "Using Investor-State Mediation Rules to Promote Conflict Management: An Introductory Guide," Washington & Lee Legal Studies Paper No. 2014-13, February 2014, 14.
[21] U.S. Court of Federal Claims, "Table G-2B: Judgments and Appeals for the 12-Month Period Ending September 30, 2012," http://www.uscourts.gov/uscourts/Statistics/JudicialBusiness/2012/appendices/G02BSep12.pdf.
[22] Richard E. Moberly, "Unfulfilled Expectations: An Empirical Analysis of Why Sarbanes-Oxley Whistleblowers Rarely Win," *William & Mary Law Review* 49, issue 1 (2007); Richard E. Moberly, "Sarbanes-Oxley's Whistleblower Provisions: Ten Years Later," *South Carolina Law Review* 64, no. 1 (2012); Nancy M. Modesitt, "Why Whistleblowers Lose: An Empirical and Qualitative Analysis of State Court Cases," *Kansas Law Review* 62, no. 1 (2013).
[23] David Freeman Engstrom, "Harnessing the Private Attorney General: Evidence from Qui Tam Litigation," *Columbia Law Review* 112, issue 6 (2012).
[24] Alexander A. Reinert, "Measuring the Success of *Bivens* Litigation and Its Consequences for the Individual Liability Model," *Stanford Law Review* 62 (2010).
[25] Michael A. Carrier and Daryl Wander, "Citizens Petitions: An Empirical Study," *Cardozo Law Review* 34 (2012); see also William N. Eskridge Jr. and Lauren E. Baer, "The Continuum of Deference: Supreme Court Treatment of Agency Statutory Interpretations from Chevron to Hamdan," *Georgetown Law Journal* 96 (2008).
[26] Thomas H. Cohen, "Tort Bench and Jury Trials in State Courts, 2005," *Bureau of Justice Statistics Bulletin*, November 2009, 4, http://1.usa.gov/1bJn8Mt; David A. Hyman and Charles Silver, "Medical Malpractice Litigation and Tort Reform: It's the Incentives, Stupid," *Vanderbilt Law Review* 59, no. 4 (2006).

Figure 7: Average Claim vs. Average Award in U.S. dollars (thousands)

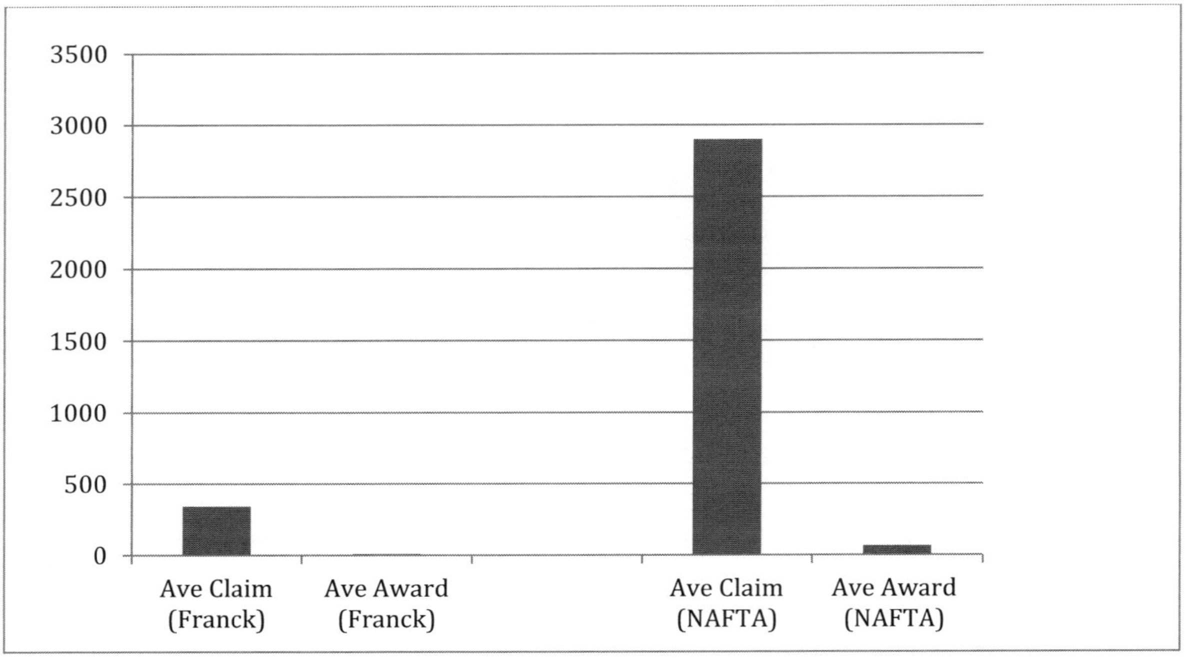

doctrinally similar to ISDS as they involve claims by individuals, claims against a state, claims related to improper regulatory activity, or claims seeking compensation.

Professor Franck's study showed that the range of damage awards was quite large. The smallest award amount was nearly US$25,000, and the largest was US$270 million. Tribunals awarded more than $10 million in 4 out of 25 arbitration claims in which the investor prevailed. In 4 other disputes, tribunals awarded between US$5 and US$10 million, and in the remaining 13, the awards were less than US$5 million. Tribunals, Franck noted, rarely found in favor of the claimant on all causes of action.[27]

The evidence from completed arbitrations fits with what many commentators have noted about the character of investor-state disputes serving as a "last resort" for investors. Especially in the circumstances of individuals and small firms, investors undertake the large expense and poor odds because the alternative (bankruptcy, or abandoning expropriated assets) is worse. An investor today deciding whether or not to enter ISDS would certainly be aware of the high costs and distant, small benefits of arbitration. But, as we will discuss in the next section, other factors exist that, on balance, deter investors from entering an international investment dispute in the first place.

[27] Franck, "Empirically Evaluating Claims about Investment Treaty Arbitration," 58–60.

Can an Investor Use ISDS to Overturn Laws or Regulation?

BITs do not grant ISDS tribunals the authority to overturn national legislation or regulations. Treaties are explicit about the available remedies for investors, and most BITs limit arbitral panels to compensation for a treaty breach. Article 34 of the U.S. Model BIT, for instance, limits awards to monetary damages and restitution of property.[1]

On occasion, states have chosen to rescind regulations as part of settlements negotiated to resolve ISDS disputes. For example, in the NAFTA case brought by Ethyl Corporation, Canada chose to rescind regulations that were separately found to violate inter-provincial laws when they settled the dispute prior to a panel decision.[2]

The vast majority of investor claims do not challenge the government's power to legislate or regulate. Rather, they challenge the government's administration of law and regulation, such as a government's treatment of an individual investor in the context of a particular license, permit, or promise extended by government officials.

Direct challenges to the government's legislative or regulatory powers have occasionally been made, but have always been unsuccessful. In the NAFTA case Chemtura v. Canada, the investor challenged Canadian pesticide regulations. The tribunal ruled against Chemtura on all claims and the panel expressly recognized Canada's right to make scientific and environmental regulatory decisions.[3] In another NAFTA case, Methanex v. United States, the tribunal dismissed all of Methanex's claims of discriminatory treatment and expropriation, noting that "as a matter of general international law, a nondiscriminatory regulation for a public purpose, which is enacted in accordance with due process and affects foreign investors, 'is not deemed expropriatory and compensable unless specific commitment had been given by the regulating government to the then putative foreign investor contemplating investment that the government would refrain from such regulation.'"[4]

Finally, there is no evidence that any government has changed a policy position or refrained from acting in a policy area for fear of potential ISDS claims. To the contrary, many BITs (including all U.S. agreements since 2004) stipulate that "except in rare circumstances, non-discriminatory regulatory actions that are designed and applied to protect legitimate public welfare objectives . . . do not constitute an indirect expropriation."[5]

---

[1] U.S. Department of State, "2012 U.S. Model Bilateral Investment Treaty," 36, http://www.state.gov/documents/organization/188371.pdf.
[2] Christian Tietje and Freya Baetens, "The Impact of Investor-State-Dispute Settlement (ISDS) in the Transatlantic Trade and Investment Partnership," June 24, 2014, 43, 79–80, http://www.investmentpolicycentral.com/sites/g/files/g798796/f/201409/the-impact-of-investor-state-dispute-settlement-isds-in-the-ttip%20%281%29.pdf.
[3] Ibid., 83.
[4] Ibid., 84.
[5] U.S. Department of State, "2012 U.S. Model Bilateral Investment Treaty," 41.

How Do Investors Pursue ISDS Cases?

Filing an ISDS claim is a serious decision. Investors sink substantial amounts into buying or leasing land, building new facilities, establishing relationships, and recruiting and training employees. These expenditures are based on calculations that predict recovery of those costs and earning of profits over time. Once a decision to establish operations is taken, the enterprise operates as a "going concern." Management decisionmaking focuses on keeping the business operating; in the event of a problem with the host government, the first instinct is to seek to reach a settlement or understanding that allows continuing operations.

A key factor in any decision to litigate or seek arbitration is the scale of an expropriation or other government mistreatment, which could range from a narrowing of business opportunities that reduce current revenue and expected earnings to a taking of the established capital stock along with all prospect of revenue and profits. The first scenario can still be quite serious—a narrowing of business opportunities could make it impossible for the company to recover its initial investment.

The ISDS process begins with formally notifying the host government of the existence and nature of a treaty breach. The next phase, required by almost every BIT, is a "cooling-off" period, from three to six months, to give the disputants an opportunity to resolve the matter through negotiation, consultation, or other alternative. During this period, the foreign investor may enlist diplomatic support from his own government, but once a claim proceeds to ICSID arbitration, the investor's government is precluded from intervening on his behalf. (Other systems do not expressly forbid intervention by the investor's government, but the practice of nonintervention has become customary.)

Since the host government could interpret the filing of an ISDS claim as a public accusation of theft, an investor must consider the probability of retaliation. Governments could further limit the scope of the company's activities, up to and including the possible termination of the company's access to a given country's markets. Occidental Petroleum faced this exact scenario in Ecuador. In 2004, Occidental won an ICSID arbitration award of US$75 million against Ecuador as compensation for unpaid value added tax (VAT) refunds. Two years later, Ecuador terminated Occidental's participation contract, for which an ICSID arbitration panel awarded Occidental an additional US$1.77 billion in compensation in 2012.[28] In another dispute, an investor chose to file an ISDS claim only when it became clear that it faced a choice to either arbitrate or declare bankruptcy for the entire company.

Once the investor submits a claim to arbitration, it remains the driver of the process, but it has multiple gates that must be passed before consideration of the claims on their merits takes place. If, after submitting the claim, the investor withdraws it, the process stops. After filing a claim, the investor must pay a deposit to the arbitral institution to underwrite the costs of the process, and it must nominate an arbitrator. While the state respondent must match these steps, if the investor fails to make this payment or fails to appoint an arbitrator, the process ceases. The final hurdle is convincing the arbitrators that they have jurisdiction to review the merits of the claim. For American companies using ICSID for ISDS arbitration, one in eight fails to pass this last test.

The arbitration process involves not only the main proceedings, but also any challenges to the arbitral award that may be pursued. An arbitration generally takes an average of three and a half years,[29] but some arbitrations have taken longer. Given experience to date, investors can develop a clear understanding of the performance of the system relative to other options. The record of dispute resolution outcomes, damage award values, award amounts, relative costs, time taken to resolve claims, and available legal counsel and arbitrators would presumably all be factored into an investor's decision to file a claim.

---

[28] Damon Vis-Dunbar, "US$1.76 billion dollar award levied against Ecuador in dispute with Occidental; tribunal split over damages," *Investment Treaty News*, January 14, 2013, http://www.iisd.org/itn/2013/01/14/awards-and-decisions-10/.

[29] Franck, "Using Investor-State Mediation Rules to Promote Conflict Management," 12.

Costs for engaging in ISDS are substantial. The Organization for Economic Cooperation and Development (OECD) has estimated that they average US$8 million and have occasionally exceeded US$30 million.[30] In addition, Professor Franck noted that in nearly 40 percent of the awards she studied, tribunals have occasionally required that claimants cover an average of US$900,000 of respondents' legal fees. Fees charged to pay tribunal and administrative costs average US$600,000.[31]

Despite the evidence that states tend to prevail in arbitrations, investors continue to file ISDS claims. In many circumstances, investors view ISDS as a better option than a lawsuit in host-nation courts or ignoring the treaty violation. Two factors appear to underlie this behavior. ISDS at least provides investors with the semblance of a level playing field, but it also provides them with a final resolution. Host governments cannot draw out the resolution process through appeals to higher courts. In addition, finality and the international publicity associated with the filing of a claim create leverage to negotiate a settlement, an outcome that occurs one-third of the time.

How Governments Benefit from Dispute Arbitration

Over the past 50 years, governments have made a strong policy commitment to BITs with ISDS, one treaty at a time, to achieve today's network of investor protection agreements. The modern BIT has received wide acceptance by states of all sizes and all levels of development primarily because it is a superior instrument versus the alternatives. BITs deliver important, treaty-based assurance to investors regarding decent treatment, and they operate in a peaceful, de-politicized manner that represents a vast improvement over espousal and gunboat diplomacy. While capital-exporting states originally endorsed BITs to protect their investors abroad, in today's circumstances every economy is both capital importer and capital exporter. Evidence from arbitration indicates that even G7 members act in ways that amount to a treaty violation, and fair adjudication will mean that states will be both winners and losers in arbitration.

Implementing an international agreement that, once operating, delivers surprising outcomes is not new. Consider the early days of the World Trade Organization's (WTO) binding dispute settlement understanding (DSU). Some U.S. elected officials who had championed the DSU after years of frustration with the General Agreement on Tariffs and Trade's (GATT) nonbinding system were shocked to find that U.S. trade law and regulation could violate the GATT, as happened in 1997 when Venezuela prevailed in the "reformulated gasoline" dispute. At the time, surprise translated into calls for reform, which ultimately did not succeed because of the complexity of modifying GATT rules. Now, 20 years after the DSU's founding, member economies have more reasonable expectations about winning and losing, and the WTO's decisions are respected by members.

The BIT network would be much easier to unwind in the name of "reform" than the WTO: bilateral treaties can be renegotiated or abrogated outright, and future negotiating objectives can be changed to emphasize the defensive interests of the state, at the

---

30 Organization for Economic Cooperation and Development (OECD), Investor State Dispute Settlement: Public Consultation, 16 May–9 July 2012 (Paris: OECD, 2012), 18, http://www.oecd.org/investment/internationalinvestmentagreements/50291642.pdf.

31 Franck, "Empirically Evaluating Claims about Investment Treaty Arbitration," 67–70; and Susan D. Franck, "Rationalizing Costs in Investment Treaty Arbitration," *Washington University Law Review* 88, no. 4 (2011).

expense of fair treatment for the investor. A lost arbitration does not necessarily mean the treaty or the arbitral panel were flawed; sometimes, states lose arbitrations because they acted in a way that breached their obligations. Our recommendation is that governments carefully review actual outcomes before implementing “reforms” to the BIT that effectively limit or reverse the protections that encourage firms to invest in their economies.

Appendix 1. Investment Policy: From "Gunboat Diplomacy" to BITs

If a country's private outward foreign direct investment (FDI) and international commercial activity enhance its foreign policy by projecting national power, prestige, economic vitality, and values, then in the often zero-sum world of international relations, the nationalization/expropriation of a foreign investment detracts from the FDI source country's power, prestige, and economic vitality. Consequently, states have gone to great lengths, including the use of military force, to protect private outward investment and private international commercial interests. The United States is no exception to this pattern.

In 1805, U.S. Naval agent to the Barbary Powers Captain William Eaton, Navy Lieutenant John Dent, eight U.S. Marines, and approximately 400 European and Arab mercenaries captured the Libyan town of Derna, and "to the shores of Tripoli" entered the Marines' Hymn.[1] More importantly, the ruler of Tripoli agreed to end his piracy of American ships and to free American prisoners.[2]

For the first time in its history, the United States had successfully intervened militarily in a foreign country to defend Americans' private international commercial interests. Over the next 160 years, the U.S. government would order its military forces to intervene in foreign countries 88 times (48 percent of all U.S. foreign military interventions during the period) to protect Americans' private international commercial interests. Perhaps the most significant of these deployments was the decades-long stationing of between 3,000 and 5,000 American soldiers and sailors in China between 1900 and 1941.[3]

The practice was glorified as "gunboat diplomacy." President Theodore Roosevelt talked of "speaking softly and carrying a big stick," and he formulated the "Roosevelt Corollary" to the Monroe Doctrine that asserted a U.S. right to intervene militarily in Central American and Caribbean countries to "stabilize" their economies if they could not pay their international debts. However, frequent application of the Roosevelt corollary in the twentieth century inspired growing anger in Latin American populations, complicating American diplomacy in the region for decades.[4] By 1970, "gunboat diplomacy" had been thoroughly discredited.

Parallel to the policy of military intervention in weaker countries to protect the private international commercial (both trade and investment) interests of American citizens, the

---

[1] "First Barbary War (1801–1805)," *American History Central*, 2014, http://www.americanhistorycentral.com/entry.php?rec=468; and Gerald W. Gawalt, "America and the Barbary Pirates: An International Battle Against an Unconventional Foe," Thomas Jefferson Papers, Library of Congress, http://memory.loc.gov/ammem/collections/jefferson_papers/mtjprece.html.

[2] "Barbary Wars, 1801–1805 and 1815–1816," Office of the Historian, Department of State, https://history.state.gov/milestones/1801-1829/barbary-wars.

[3] "Timeline of United States Military Operations," Wikipedia, http://en.wikipedia.org/wiki/Timeline_of_United_States_military_operations.

[4] Kenneth J. Vandevelde, "A Brief History of International Investment Agreements," *U.C.-Davis Journal of International Law & Policy* 12, no. 1 (2005): 161.

United States sought to protect such interests in stronger countries through the negotiation of Treaties of Friendship, Commerce, and Navigation (FCN). America's first FCN treaty was concluded in 1778 with France, followed by treaties with the Netherlands (1782), Sweden (1783), and Prussia (1785).[5] In 1794, the Treaty of Amity, Commerce, and Navigation with Great Britain established mixed Anglo-American arbitration commissions to resolve boundary disputes and claims from British and American citizens for property lost during the Revolutionary War. This was the first treaty to provide for mixed commissions to resolve disputes between individuals and states. Thus, the Founders of America who negotiated, provided senatorial advice and consent, and ratified this treaty "provided an important blueprint for international investment treaties and the investor-state arbitration system in place today."[6]

As U.S. outward foreign direct investment increased in the twentieth century, the United States progressively strengthened property rights protections in FCN treaty texts. Early versions provided basic rights to establish a business and to settle disputes before host nations' courts. Post–World War II versions of the FCN included most of the rights found in today's BITs, including provisions that the parties would not take foreign investors' property without due process and prompt and just compensation. In addition, they provided a remedy to expropriation without compensation; state parties could "espouse" claims and submit disputes to the International Court of Justice (ICJ) for resolution.[7]

Despite some successes, the state-to-state process proved both inefficient and unsatisfactory. Positively, state-versus-state lawsuits before the ICJ established key precedents in international law on the protection of foreign investment, including the concepts of a minimum standard of treatment for foreign investors and the obligation of states to award compensation for private property seized from foreign nationals. On the other hand, the ICJ's requirement that claimants exhaust all local legal remedies before it would accept a suit and states' necessarily adopting this standard into their own procedures for "espousing" a case frustrates claimants both in terms of cost and time. Espousal has also been an irritant to bilateral relations, whether states seek to negotiate mutually satisfactory solutions or bring the matter before an international tribunal.[8]

The Cold War era, characterized by its bipolarity and high-risk international competition, but also by significant global foreign direct investment growth, stimulated a game-changing innovation in international relations and international law, the bilateral investment treaty (BIT). The BIT combined the stronger investment rights of the new FCN treaties with a new remedy for treaty violations, investor-state dispute settlement (ISDS).

---

[5] John F. Coyle, "The Treaty of Friendship, Commerce, and Navigation in the Modern Era," *Columbia Journal of Transnational Law* 51 (2013): 307.
[6] Christian Tietje and Freya Baetens, "The Impact of Investor-State-Dispute Settlement (ISDS) in the Transatlantic Trade and Investment Partnership," June 24, 2014, 18, http://www.investmentpolicycentral.com/sites/g/files/g798796/f/201409/the-impact-of-investor-state-dispute-settlement-isds-in-the-ttip%20%281%29.pdf.
[7] Wayne Sachs, "The New U.S. Bilateral Investment Treaties," *Berkeley Journal of International Law* 2, issue 1 (1984): 198–219; Vandevelde, "A Brief History of International Investment Agreements," 162–66; and Coyle, "The Treaty of Friendship, Commerce, and Navigation in the Modern Era," 307–08, 313–15.
[8] Vandevelde, "A Brief History of International Investment Agreements," 165, 169.

More efficient and less costly for all parties, ISDS has effectively replaced the cumbersome and consistently unsatisfactory state-to-state dispute resolution system while also virtually eliminating the practice of “gunboat diplomacy” to resolve investment disputes.

Appendix 2. The Evolution of the U.S. Model BIT

The United States adopted the bilateral investment treaty (BIT) as its primary investment policy tool in 1982, with the completion of the U.S.-Egypt BIT and simultaneous establishment of a U.S. "model" text. All U.S. treaties of Friendship, Commerce, and Navigation (FCN) contained protections for U.S. investors, beginning with the Jay Treaty of 1794 with Great Britain. But the Model BIT of 1982 improved upon investor protection provisions contained in post–World War II FCN treaties. Further, for the first time the BIT provided U.S. investors access to neutral arbitration at the International Centre for Settlement of Investment Disputes (ICSID) as an alternative to local courts (later expanded to include the United Nations Commission on International Trade Law, or UNCITRAL, rules and other forms of international arbitration).[1] Of the 41 U.S. BITs currently in force, 28 of them are based on the core concepts found in this initial text.[2]

One major policy innovation of the new U.S. BIT was the inclusion of "pre-establishment" obligations, which effectively opened foreign markets to U.S. investors (in addition to protecting the investments they had already established). The text expanded coverage to investors "in the process of committing substantial capital or other resources to an investment," broadened the definition of "investment," and obligated host states to provide the better of "national treatment" (NT) or "most-favored nation" (MFN) treatment to incoming investment from the United States. Additionally, the new treaties established an external legal standard for the principle of "fair and equitable" treatment for foreign investors: covered investments would be treated no less favorably than required by customary international law.[3]

Based on the free-flow-of-capital principles found in the Organization for Economic Cooperation and Development (OECD) Codes of Liberalization of Capital Movements, the new U.S. BIT guaranteed investors' access to local capital markets and their right to transfer capital freely into and out of host countries regardless of their capital control policies.[4] Further, the BIT's explicit protections against losses from expropriation, war, or civil strife, and the elaboration of the "prompt, adequate, and effective" standard for compensation, combined effectively with other treaty provisions to protect American investors' property interests in the territory of a BIT partner, regardless of the form of investment.[5]

The addition of investor-state dispute settlement (ISDS) gave investors substantial control over the dispute resolution process within the range of alternatives, a major improvement over the FCN treaties. Investors' access to binding investor-state

---

[1] Wayne Sachs, "The New U.S. Bilateral Investment Treaties," *Berkeley Journal of International Law* 2, issue 1 (1984): 194.
[2] U.S. Department of State, "United States Bilateral Investment Treaties," http://www.state.gov/e/eb/ifd/bit/117402.htm.
[3] Sachs, "The New U.S. Bilateral Investment Treaties," 194.
[4] Ibid., 195.
[5] Ibid., 214.

arbitration came through a BIT provision in which the treaty parties agreed in advance to the jurisdiction of relevant arbitral process once an investor files a claim with that entity.[6] The BIT text's broad definition of "investment dispute" created an important incentive for state parties to ensure reasonable treatment of the foreign investor and its covered investment.

In 1994, the United States developed a revised Model BIT text that introduced new provisions and clarified existing measures in ways that yielded a net strengthening of investor rights and protections. While the new text introduced the term "covered investment" to refer to those investments that are subject to the treaty's terms, the definition covered essentially all assets found on an investor's balance sheet. Among the largest changes was an expanded list of prohibited performance requirements and new disciplines on state enterprises. The new text clarified the process for calculating compensation for expropriation in an economy with a nonconvertible currency. It expanded the text on compensation for damages due to war and other forms of coercion by including a requirement to provide restitution for losses from requisitioning or destruction by a party. The article on transfers was reconfigured, and contained a new specification guaranteeing that covered investments could make transfers in kind consistent with their agreements with a party, although it also identified circumstances under which a party might prevent a covered investment from transferring resources outside a party's territory.[7]

The dispute settlement sections of the 1994 text also represented an improvement for investors. The waiting period to file for binding arbitration was reduced from six to three months. Meanwhile, the text enabled the investor to seek injunctive relief from an expropriation in host-country courts whether or not the investor had filed for arbitration (referred to as the "no U-turn" clause). The obligation on a party to enforce an arbitral award in its own territory was mandated as the text was changed to "shall carry out without delay" from "undertake to carry out." On the other hand, the ability to claim expropriation through taxation was limited by a mandatory review by both parties' tax authorities. A dispute could not proceed if both tax authorities agreed that an expropriation had not occurred.[8]

The 1994 Model had been the basis of 11 new treaties[9] as well as the investment chapter of the North American Free Trade Agreement (NAFTA). In 2001, U.S. investment policy became a topic of intense debate in the U.S. Congress, leading to a set of specific policy objectives for investment incorporated in the Trade Act of 2002. Upon enactment, the United States suspended BIT negotiations and reviewed its Model BIT.[10] The purpose of the review was to conform the U.S. Model BIT to the investment directives of the Trade Act of 2002, but the debate in Congress and within the administration was influenced in

---

[6] Ibid., 221.
[7] "Azerbaijan Bilateral Investment Treaty," 106th Congress, 2nd session, http://2001-2009.state.gov/documents/organization/43478.pdf.
[8] Ibid.
[9] U.S. Department of State, "United States Bilateral Investment Treaties," http://www.state.gov/e/eb/ifd/bit/117402.htm.
[10] Kenneth J. Vandevelde, "Model Bilateral Investment Treaties: The Way Forward," *Southwestern Journal of International Law* 18 (2011): 308–09.

large measure by defensive concerns resulting from arbitration claims being filed by Canadian investors against the United States using NAFTA's investment chapter.[11]

The final product of the review, the 2004 Model BIT, substantially strengthened state prerogatives in a manner that arguably reduced investor rights and protections. The new text granted new exceptions for prudential measures related to financial services regulation and for monetary, credit, and exchange rate polices.[12] The 2004 text restricted coverage of the treaty's "umbrella" clause only to claims stemming from an investment agreement and not to other contractual obligations,[13] and deleted other investor-friendly provisions, for example, the "effective means of bringing claims" clause and the "arbitrary and discriminatory treatment" clause. In line with similar changes to trade policy, the text added new commitments on labor rights and environmental protection.[14] Moreover, the new text deleted an obligation that state enterprises provide the better of national treatment or MFN treatment with respect to their sale of goods and services to covered investments.[15] The 2004 Model did increase transparency requirements and expanded the list of prohibitions on performance requirements.[16]

BIT provisions related to ISDS received the lion's share of attention during the review. First, the new text clarified the meaning of key concepts, for example, fair and equitable treatment and indirect expropriation, while also providing greater detail that leaves "less room for interpretation by arbitral tribunals."[17] Fair and equitable treatment would no longer require treatment in addition to or beyond what is required by international law. The 1994 Model had set the minimum standard of treatment as exactly that, the lowest standard an investor could expect.[18] Second, the new model created mechanisms that allowed BIT parties to agree on interpretations of BIT provisions that were binding on an ISDS tribunal and that allowed a nondisputing state party to intervene in ISDS proceedings to present its interpretation of the BIT's provisions. Third, the 2004 text limited ISDS filings to claims less than three years old, extended the waiting period to file an arbitration claim from three to six months, and required abandonment of any pursuit of a claim in the courts or administrative tribunals of either party contemporaneously to filing for arbitration (the so-called fork-in-the-road provision). Finally, the new model expedited formation of arbitral panels, authorized prompt dismissal of frivolous claims, allowed consolidation of related claims, permitted the use of expert reports and *amicus curiae* submissions, and encouraged the creation of an appellate mechanism.[19]

---

[11] Ibid.
[12] Ibid., 310.
[13] Katia Yannaca-Small, "Interpretation of the Umbrella Clause in Investment Agreements," OECD Working Papers on International Investment, 2006/03, October 2006, 14, http://www.oecd.org/daf/inv/investment-policy/WP-2006_3.pdf.
[14] Vandevelde, "Model Bilateral Investment Treaties," 310–11.
[15] Comparison of the text of the "Azerbaijan Bilateral Investment Treaty," http://2001-2009.state.gov/documents/organization/43478.pdf, and the text of the "2004 Model BIT," http://www.state.gov/documents/organization/117601.pdf.
[16] Vandevelde, "Model Bilateral Investment Treaties," 311.
[17] Ibid., 310.
[18] Stephen M. Schwebel, "A Critical Assessment of the U.S. Model BIT" (keynote address at Twelfth ITF [Investment Treaty Forum] Public Conference, British Institute of International & Comparative Law, London, May 15, 2009), 8–10, http://www.biicl.org/files/4253_schwebel-biicl15may2009speech_cor2.pdf.
[19] Vandevelde, "Model Bilateral Investment Treaties," 310–11.

Figure A1: U.S. Investment Agreements by Model Text

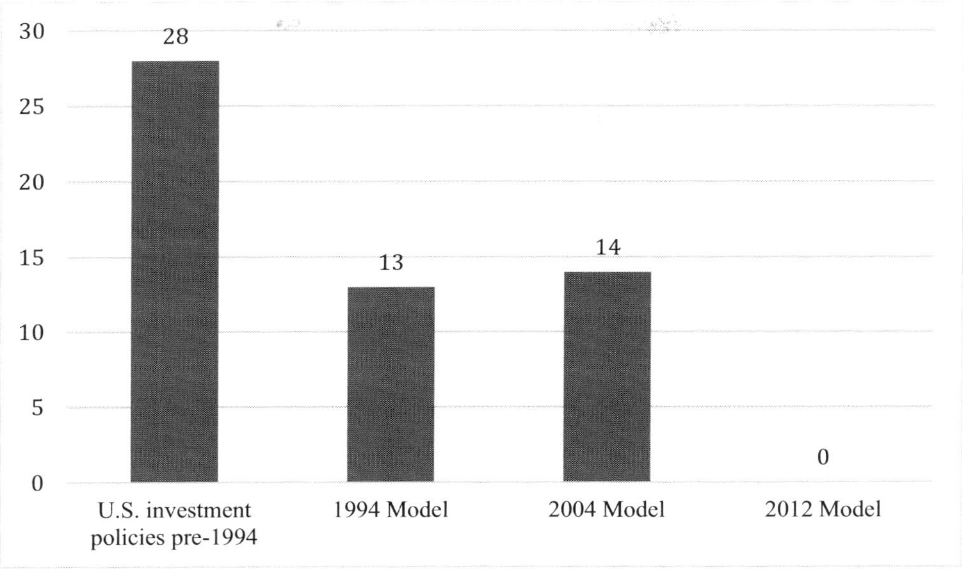

After completing two BIT negotiations (Uruguay and Rwanda) as well as free-trade agreements with investment chapters covering 12 parties based on the 2004 Model text, the U.S. again suspended BIT negotiations (with China and India, among others) in 2009 to conduct another public review of its Model BIT. Three years later, the 2012 Model BIT expanded or strengthened party obligations in three main areas—transparency and public participation, labor rights and environmental protection, and state-led economies.[20] However, the 2012 Model BIT text made no substantive changes in dispute settlement procedures. Essentially, the Obama administration ultimately agreed with the Bush and Clinton administrations that ISDS was an essential component of U.S. foreign investment policy.[21]

Through over 30 years of application and three public reviews of text led by administrations of both political parties, the model U.S. bilateral investment treaty text has evolved from an instrument to protect investment and to open markets for American investors into a diplomatic tool that also advances U.S. policy goals in labor rights, environmental policy, transparency, and more broadly, the rule of law. All three reviews determined that ISDS should remain a cornerstone feature of the U.S. Model BIT. This fact reflects a long-term, bipartisan commitment by America's political leadership to international arbitration as the preferred means for resolving investor-state disputes.

---

[20] U.S. Department of State, "United States Concludes Review of Model Bilateral Investment Treaty," media note, April 20, 2012, http://www.state.gov/r/pa/prs/ps/2012/04/188198.htm.
[21] Office of the United States Trade Representative, "The Facts on Investor-State Dispute Settlement: Safeguarding the Public Interest and Protecting Investors," March 27, 2014, http://www.ustr.gov/about-us/press-office/blog/2014/March/Facts-Investor-State%20Dispute-Settlement-Safeguarding-Public-Interest-Protecting-Investors.

| Appendix 3. Conference Proceedings

On October 31, 2014, the CSIS Scholl Chair hosted a conference entitled "Investor-State Dispute Settlement: A Reality Check," which presented Professor Susan Franck's preliminary findings from research into investor-state arbitration, followed by an expert panel that discussed the various policy aspects of ISDS. A brief summary of the speakers' remarks can be found below, and the event may be viewed online at http://csis.org/event/investor-state-dispute-settlement-reality-check.

Investor-State Dispute Settlement: A Reality Check—Keynote Address

Grant Aldonas, Senior Adviser, Center for Strategic and International Studies

In the wake of the completion of the Uruguay Round and the creation of the WTO in 1994, it was clear that the one remaining gap in international commercial law related to foreign direct investment and the settlement of investor-state disputes. The subsequent 20 years, in which the nature of competition has changed dramatically, have emphasized that this gap still remains to be filled. Expanding international investment flows have outstripped even the impressive growth in world trade during that time.

The central international economic policy challenge facing the United States involves raising our productivity and improving our competitiveness. Exports alone are not the answer nor are they an adequate indicator of our economic progress. To continue to drive economic growth, we must remain at the technological frontier. That requires a broader engagement in the world economy and active participation in the global flow of knowledge and technology.

International investment offers an important means of doing just that. Indeed, it reinforces our ability to export and otherwise compete, particularly in emerging markets that will shape the world economy going forward. Obtaining those benefits, however, depends on a set of rules on investment that, like their counterparts governing world trade, reward U.S. firms and their workers for their industry, initiative, and innovation.

The benefits of closing the gap in the international economic architecture and adopting solid investment protections extend well beyond our own economic interests. Developing economies likewise need institutions that operate based on mutually agreed rules to maximize benefits from their participation in the global diffusion of knowledge and technology. Toward that end, they need strong rules that not only attract and protect foreign investment, but that reward domestic investors as well. Those include, most importantly, property rights and a fair system of enforcing contracts. International investment rules, including their dispute settlement provisions, reinforce those institutions and create an environment that fosters growth and development.

From a U.S. perspective, the benefits of adopting international investment rules, including investor-state dispute settlement, cost nothing. The substantive and procedural guarantees afforded by international investment rules, as well as the settled principles of customary international law from which they are drawn, conform to the rights provided by the Fifth Amendment protections found in our own Constitution. They do not afford foreign investors any right or process other than what they are already due under U.S. law. What they do provide is a guarantee of equal treatment before the law, establishing a basis for all countries to participate profitably in the global economy.

An Evidence-Based Approach to International Investment Law

Susan D. Franck, Professor of Law, Washington and Lee University

The analysis was based upon 272 public awards issued by investment treaty arbitration tribunals as of January 2012, of which 159 were final awards that conclusively ended a case irrespective of whether the dispute was finally resolved at jurisdiction, on the merits, or at the damages phase.

The data reflected that, for final outcomes, states won 55 percent of the cases, investors won 36 percent of the cases, and 9 percent of the cases were resolved by settlements or discontinuances. Excluding the settlements and discontinuances, proportionately, states won roughly three cases for every two cases investors won. The difference, where states won more cases than investors, was statistically meaningful.

The pattern of outcomes in final awards in investor-state arbitration was relatively stable over time. Earlier research from 2007[1] reflected a similar pattern of final outcomes, namely: states won 58 percent of the cases, investors won 38 percent of the cases, and settlements represented 4 percent of the final awards.[2] Excluding settlements, the earlier analysis reflected roughly the same state win-to-loss ratio such that, for every two cases investors won, states won three cases (2:3).

The outcomes of investment treaty cases were similar to other research that has empirically analyzed the outcomes of various types of litigation in U.S. courts. For instance, in *qui tam* litigation or litigation brought by whistleblowers, like investors' success levels, plaintiffs' success rates were comparatively low. Likewise, in cases brought against governments or government agencies, like *Bivens* claims involving alleged constitutional violations, government entities have experienced relatively high win rates.

For the 159 final awards, the mean amount claimed was around US$600 million and the mean amount awarded was just over $16 million. Looking just at those disputes where tribunals awarded investors some compensation, the average amount investors claimed

---

[1] Susan D. Franck, "Empirically Evaluating Claims about Investment Treaty Arbitration," *North Carolina Law Review* 86 (2007).
[2] Note that, in the earlier generation of research, discontinuances were not analyzed. This means that the more recent research, which incorporated discontinuances, reflects a slightly different unit of analysis.

was roughly US$171 million, and the average amount awarded was slightly less than $46 million.[3]

With respect to the nature of respondent states, whether looking at wins and losses, amounts awarded, or claimant relative success rates, when controlling for the effect of a state's democracy level, the data was unable to identify any reliable link to respondent states' development status.[4] This was true irrespective of whether a state's development status defined by membership in the Organization for Economic Cooperation and Development, the World Bank's classification, or the United Nations Development Programme's Human Development Index.

With respect to investors' identity, understanding outcomes requires a nuanced perspective. On one hand, the data showed that when cases involved either human beings or publicly listed corporations, those investors won roughly half of the cases and states won the other half. In contrast, when corporations that were privately held (i.e., not publicly listed) brought claims, those investors only won roughly one out of three cases. On the other hand, exploring investor identity as a function of whether at least one claimant (or a claimant's parent company) was listed on the *Financial Times* 500 (*FT500*) offered a different perspective. For cases involving at least one *FT500*-related investor, investors won reliably more often than states. The cases involving an *FT500*-related investor, however, were a fraction (under 10 percent) of the 159 final cases; and the results could reflect a case selection effect since it is possible that *FT500* entities may be screening cases to avoid bringing unmeritorious claims and to pursue only the most serious claims. By contrast, for the vast majority of cases that did not involve an *FT500*-related investor, states won roughly 60 percent of the cases.[5]

The data also revealed key information on time and cost: The average time from the filing of a claim to a final award was three and a half years.

Costs were substantial, particularly when compared to the average awards. On average, investors incurred US$5 million for their legal counsel, and states incurred an average cost of US$4.6 million. By comparison, administrative costs for arbitration panels were proportionately smaller and more reasonable and, on average, less than US$1 million. The data continue to reflect the historical trend that, more often than not, tribunals did not generally shift the costs incurred by legal counsel or tribunals; but this may reflect the overall pattern that, when states won (and because states won more than investors), tribunals did not shift costs.[6]

In conclusion, investment treaty arbitration is maturing. It provides key benefits to both investors and states. Some elements of investment arbitration, however, should concern the policy community. Derivative reforms should, therefore, be targeted to solve discrete

---

[3] Susan D. Franck, "Using Investor-State Mediation Rules to Promote Conflict Management: An Introductory Guide," Washington & Lee Legal Studies Paper No. 2014-13, February 2014.
[4] Susan D. Franck, "Conflating Politics and Development in the Outcomes of Investment Treaty Disputes," *Virginia Journal of International Law* (forthcoming); see also Susan D. Franck, "Development and Outcomes of Investment Treaty Arbitration," *Harvard International Law Journal* 50 (2009).
[5] Susan D. Franck, *Investment Treaty Arbitration: Myths, Realities and Costs* (New York: Oxford University Press, forthcoming).
[6] Ibid.; see also Susan D. Franck, "Rationalizing Costs in Investment Treaty Arbitration," *Washington University Law Review* 88, no. 4 (2011).

and identifiable problems so that stakeholders can solve real, rather than imagined, problems using evidence-based insights.

Trade and Investment Agreements, ISDS, and the Rule of Law

Ambassador John Veroneau, Partner, Covington and Burling LLP

In 1796, Vice-President John Adams said of the Treaty of Amity and Commerce with France that "There is no principle of the law of nations more firmly established than that which entitles the property of strangers to the protection of [the host government]."

Rule of law is a critical factor in separating desirable from undesirable countries in which to live. Who wants to live in a country where the government can expropriate one's property without compensation? The ability to prevent or redress for such abuses is a bedrock principle of the rule of law. Through trade agreements and investment treaties, the United States *inter alia* promotes rule of law by providing protection against discrimination and expropriation and a mechanism—investor-state dispute settlement (ISDS)—to resolve disputes when governments expropriate property or deny justice.

Given these fundamental contributions to the global, rules-based economy, opposition to ISDS makes little sense. Opponents of ISDS have put forward a number of questionable arguments. For instance, some assert that ISDS encourages litigation, even though relative to the stock of global foreign direct investment, the number of ISDS claims is miniscule. Others claim that ISDS prevents governments from executing their responsibilities to protect health and welfare; yet there is little factual support for this claim. Opponents of ISDS continually cite frivolous claims that have been *rejected* to support their view that ISDS bars governments from exercising legitimate regulatory powers. In fact, ISDS claims that are successful invariably reflect serious lapses in rule-of-law principles. Opponents of ISDS also claim that investment treaties convey "special rights" without acknowledging that the United States and most other countries provide similar safeguards for domestic investments at risk of expropriation.

Opponents to ISDS have also argued that investment treaties are not worth negotiating because countries cannot be counted on to uphold their commitments. This is not a compelling argument. It is better to have international rights and press for their enforcement than to lack these rights in the first instance. A more specious but candid argument offered by ISDS opponents is that the United States should view its own well-developed rule of law as a comparative advantage in the global economy and that we should not diminish this advantage by providing investment protections in countries with weak rule of law. This is a very short-sighted view. The United States has significant interests in promoting stronger rule of law in all countries through ISDS and other means.

The interests of the U.S. and global economy are served by the availability of ISDS and other tools that promote rule of law. We should continue to press for ISDS in the Transatlantic Trade and Investment Partnership (TTIP) and other international agreements.

U.S. Manufacturing and Foreign Investment: A Necessary Relationship

Linda Dempsey, Vice President, International Economic Affairs, National Association of Manufacturers

U.S. manufacturers typically make the vast majority of their investments domestically. Yet, just as companies from Europe, Asia, Latin America, and beyond invest in America to reach the American consumer, many U.S. manufacturers also need to invest overseas in order to:

- sell more successfully to the 95 percent of consumers that live outside our borders,
- access important natural resources, and
- participate in overseas infrastructure and other projects.

By reaching millions of new customers overseas and participating in foreign projects, U.S. investment overseas helps strengthen America's manufacturing base by spurring approximately 50 percent of total U.S. exports and 42 percent of manufacturing exports. In addition, these exports and the trillions of dollars in sales made by U.S. foreign affiliates support higher-paying American jobs, and very high levels of R&D and capital investment in the United States.

In making investment location decisions, manufacturers consider a number of factors including consumer market size, natural resource endowments, and location as a global hub with proximity to major markets. They also look closely at a full-range of risk, rule-of-law, and governance issues, including whether a country has agreed to high-level investment access and protections subject to neutral and impartial investor-state dispute settlement. These facts are not lost on the many countries that lack market size and geographic attributes that are still trying to appeal to foreign investing manufacturers, including many European countries that are actively supporting inclusion of investor rights and investor-state dispute settlement in the Transatlantic Trade and Investment Partnership agreement.

Foreign investors and host nations generally work well together, because both want the investments to succeed. However, occasionally problems appear, and the most prominent are incidents when host governments act either to destroy or curtail a foreign investment via outright expropriation, discrimination in favor of domestic companies, mistreatment of the foreign investor, or revocation of a license, permit, contract, or other promise. Even in such circumstances, the first order of business of investors is to try to resolve the issue by talking directly with the foreign government, U.S. government, and others. Filing an investor-state arbitration claim against a state is a step that is never taken precipitously or until other options to resolve a dispute of this magnitude have been exhausted. Even where companies want to move forward with an ISDS claim, they seriously consider that it is a costly choice in terms of both time and money, that the probability of a favorable outcome is low, and that the amount awarded is typically substantially less than the losses the foreign investor has incurred.

There is no doubt that manufacturers in the United States are facing intense competition and an unlevel playing field in many markets overseas. For manufacturing in the United States to continue to grow, we need to ensure that manufacturers and their property overseas have concrete protections and the possibility of effective and fair enforcement of foreign government obligations undertaken in our trade and investment agreements. In short, strong provisions that open and protect investment—subject to ISDS—are a critical part of a robust, pro-manufacturing policy for the United States and for any country that is globally engaged and wants to grow its manufacturing and promote stronger economic activities for its citizens.

Investor-State Dispute Settlement: It's All in the Balance of Interests

Stanimir Alexandrov, Partner, Sidley Austin LLP

Each dispute that comes before an arbitration tribunal is unique. To evaluate a claim on its merits, arbitrators read and assess thousands of pages of evidence submitted by the parties. At the end of this process, there is usually very little disagreement between the arbitrators as to the facts of the dispute. Thus, it should be no surprise that nearly all awards are unanimous.

Arbitration is driven by a balance-of-interests analysis of the facts, in part because the treaties that are the source of the claims are, as negotiated instruments, also based on a balance of interests. The analysis applies to investment treaty concepts such as fair and equitable treatment, non-discrimination, and non-arbitrariness.

There is an assertion that ISDS, per se, imposes a chill on a government's ability to regulate. However, ISDS does not really impose any more "regulatory chill" on a government's regulatory action than any other mechanism or form of litigation in other forums: international, such as the WTO, or national, such as domestic courts.

Much is made of the alleged "regulatory chill" resulting from the investment treaties' requirement that the assets of investors should not be expropriated without compensation. But this requirement is not different from the requirements or protections of property interests in domestic law. Indeed, every time the U.S. government exercises eminent domain, it has to comply with the requirements of the Fifth Amendment, including the due process, public purpose, and compensation obligations. These rights and protections are coextensive with the rights guaranteed to foreigners by BITs and trade agreements. In reality, ISDS imposes a chill on government's ability to "misregulate," that is, to act in an arbitrary, discriminatory, unfair, and inequitable manner.

It is also incorrect that the mere fact that foreign investors are permitted to assert claims in international arbitration against sovereigns imposes a "chill" on the sovereigns' ability to regulate. The system of ISDS strongly discourages investors from submitting frivolous claims. The data shows both the lower probability of investors' success in ISDS and the small amounts of compensation awarded relative to damages claimed by the investors. This demonstrates that arbitrators are fair-minded; it also causes investors to consider carefully the balance of risks associated with filing an ISDS claim against any host government and discourages them from initiating unsubstantiated or weak claims.

The statistical information shows that states win cases more often than investors. But the statistical information does not provide the full picture. In a conventional analysis, the investor wins if the investor receives a check, and the state wins if no check is issued. In reality, arbitration outcomes should be measured against each party's expectations. A recently resolved dispute is illustrative. A state revamped its energy markets to allow greater competition and decided to cancel concession contracts granted under the old regulatory regime. As expected by the government, one foreign concessionaire filed an ISDS claim asking for over US$100 million in damages. When the final award of less than US$10 million in compensation was announced, the government issued a triumphant press release while the company expressed its displeasure with the award. Technically, the investor won and the government lost, but the government perceived the outcome as very favorable and the investor—as rather unfavorable.

In sum, ISDS is a well-balanced dispute resolution mechanism that serves the interests of participants and preserves the balance of interests between them and within the treaties that are the basis for claims. While any system can be improved, proposed changes should always be carefully considered relative to the existing balance of interests within the system.

About the Authors

Scott Miller is a senior adviser and holds the William M. Scholl Chair in International Business at CSIS. From 1997 to 2012, Mr. Miller was director for global trade policy at Procter & Gamble, a leading consumer products company. In that position, he was responsible for the full range of international trade, investment, and business facilitation issues for the company. Mr. Miller has led many campaigns supporting U.S. free trade agreements, and as a member of numerous business associations, he has been a key contributor to international trade and investment policy. He advised the U.S. government as liaison to the U.S. Trade Representative's Advisory Committee for Trade Policy and Negotiations, as well as the State Department's Advisory Committee on International Economic Policy. Mr. Miller was the founding chairman of the Department of Commerce's Industry Trade Advisory Committee (ITAC) Investment Working Group. Earlier in his career, he was a manufacturing, marketing, and government relations executive for Procter & Gamble in the United States and Canada.

Mr. Miller was appointed to the Scholl Chair in August 2012. He holds a B.A. from Ohio Northern University and an M.A. from the University of Cincinnati College of Design, Architecture, Art, and Planning.

Gregory N. Hicks is a visiting fellow from the State Department where he focuses on investment policy. In the course of a 22-year career at the State Department, he has served in six overseas assignments in Libya, Afghanistan, Bahrain, Yemen, Syria, and The Gambia. During tours in Washington, D.C., he served as deputy director of the Office of Investment Affairs in the Bureau of Economic and Business Affairs, as special assistant to the under secretary of state for economic, energy, and agricultural affairs, as a trade policy negotiator for the Office of the U.S. Trade Representative, and as country officer for Vietnam, Oman, and Yemen. He played key roles in the negotiation of Vietnam's World Trade Organization (WTO) accession, the Bahrain Free Trade Agreement, the Vietnam Bilateral Trade Agreement, and Oman's WTO accession. In the course of his career, he has received six Meritorious Service Increases, four individual Superior Honor Awards, three individual Meritorious Honor Awards, and was runner-up for the department-wide Annual Human Rights Award. Prior to joining the Foreign Service, Mr. Hicks earned two master's degrees from the University of Michigan, in applied economics and modern Near Eastern and North African studies. He graduated from Bethany College, West Virginia, with a B.A. in interdisciplinary studies.

Mr. Hicks is a State Department visiting fellow at CSIS in Washington, D.C. He is writing in a personal capacity, and the views expressed in this report are entirely his own.